CONTENTS

The species depicted in this book are arranged according to genus as follows:

Genus *Protea*	2
'Mountain rose' group	6
Summer-rainfall proteas	7
Dwarf proteas	8
Genus *Leucadendron*	10
Genus *Leucospermum*	14
Genus *Mimetes*	18
Other genera	20
Serruria, Spatalla,	
Sorocephalus	20
Aulax, Diastella, Vexatorella,	
Brabejum, Paranomus,	
Orothamnus, Faurea	22
Animal pollination	24

GENUS *PROTEA*

In South Africa, *Protea* itself, with 83 species, is the largest, most flamboyant and best-known genus. Impressed by its diversity of form, the 18th-century Swedish botanist, Linnaeus, named the genus after Proteus, a god in Greek mythology who was able to assume different shapes at will. The aptness of the name is borne out not only by its growth habit, which ranges from dwarf shrubs with subterranean stems to trees in savannah woodland, but also by marked differences in the size and shape of the flower heads. It is, however, these that command most attention, ranging from the smallest, of *P. odorata* (a mere 20-30 millimetres in diameter), to the massive heads of the largest species, *P. cynaroides*, which may be up to 30 centimetres in diameter. 'Flower' is, in fact, something of a misnomer, for the part referred to is actually a compound structure consisting of hundreds of small individual flowers massed together and enclosed by a cup of brightly coloured bracts to form a goblet-shaped flower head.

In species like *P. sulphurea* from the Montagu, Worcester and Witteberg Mountains, the flower head is a shallow bowl surrounded by smooth bracts, while *P. magnifica* and *P. holosericea* have heavily bearded bracts. The former is an important ornamental species. It is also the parent of many fine hybrid selections raised for the cut-flower trade.

Both *P. lacticolour* and *P. punctata* are summer-and-autumn-flowering species from high elevations. The former has smooth, hairless leaves and is restricted to the moist, coastal Hottentots Holland and Riviersonderend mountains, while the latter has hairy leaves and favours the arid inland ranges, where it occurs from the Cederberg to Uniondale.

Though of little decorative value, the familiar *waboom* (wagon tree), *P. nitida*, is widespread in the south western and southern Cape. It was once a source of timber for the manufacture of wagon wheels and simple kitchen utensils.

1. *P. lacticolor*

2. *P. holosericea*

3. *P. punctata*

nitida (waboom)

sulphurea

6. *P. magnifica*

3

1. *P. neriifolia*

2. *P. repens* (sugar bush)

3. *P. stokoei*

4. *P. aristata*

rupicola

Protea neriifolia and the common sugar bush, *P. repens*, are two of the most wide-ranging and frequently encountered species in the south western and southern Cape. Both vary greatly in flowering times and colour, according to their locality. Certain colour variations have therefore become important elements in the year-round cut-flower trade. In the 18th and 19th centuries. *P. repens* was valued as a source of nectar from which a thick syrup, *bossiestroop*, was prepared. To make *bossiestroop*, hundreds of open flower heads were gathered and the copious nectar shaken out into a suitable container. Later it was strained, boiled and finally bottled for use as a sugar substitute, or for treating coughs and other chest complaints.

The other species on these pages are less frequently seen in their natural habitats. *Protea stokoei* is a rarity from the high, cool, perpetually moist summits of the Hottentots Holland and Kogelberg mountains. Conversely, *P. aristata* is endemic to the arid Klein Swartberg, its pine-needle-like leaves being a particularly distinctive feature. *Protea grandiceps* frequents the uppermost peaks of the major coastal ranges between Cape Town and Port Elizabeth, but, unlike other members of its genus from high elevations, it has taken well to cultivation and is now frequently seen in gardens. The rock dweller, *P. rupicola*, occupies a habitat parallel to *P. grandiceps*, rooting itself among boulders on the most exposed summits of the drier inland mountains from Tulbagh to Port Elizabeth. As a result, these species are seldom seen *in situ* except by mountaineers or energetic hikers.

grandiceps

'MOUNTAIN ROSE' PROTEAS

The species figured on this page all have small to medium-sized, dark-red, pendulous flower heads and, perhaps inevitably, are known by the vernacular names *skaamblom* (shy flower) or 'mountain rose'. Best known among this appealing group is *Protea nana*, a small shrub with needle-like leaves. A winter-flowering species, it is occasionally encountered in the Du Toit's Kloof, Wolseley, Tulbagh and Ceres mountains. *Protea witzenbergiana* is closely related, but has a sprawling, almost prostrate mode of growth and minute hairs on its spine-tipped leaves. It is found on the Ceres mountains and throughout the Kouebokkeveld to the southern Cederberg.

Both *P. pendula* and *P. effusa* are larger, broad-leaved shrubs from the Kouebokkeveld and Ceres mountains, attaining two metres when mature. Despite their size, they are invariably overlooked, as their distinctive blooms are frequently concealed within a mass of foliage.

1. *P. pityphylla*

2. *P. nana*

3. *P. pendula*

4. *P. witzenbergiana*

5. *P. effusa*

caffra

dracomontana

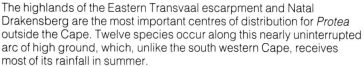

8. *P. roupelliae*

SUMMER-RAINFALL PROTEAS

The highlands of the Eastern Transvaal escarpment and Natal Drakensberg are the most important centres of distribution for *Protea* outside the Cape. Twelve species occur along this nearly uninterrupted arc of high ground, which, unlike the south western Cape, receives most of its rainfall in summer.

In the Natal Drakensberg, *P. caffra* and *P. roupelliae* are the most abundant species. Both attain the stature of small trees and are commonest on soils derived from Cave-Sandstone rocks, where they are often sufficiently abundant to form a sparse, open woodland At higher elevations, the dwarf *P. dracomontana*, a Drakensberg endemic, grows socially on the heavier basaltic soils in a zone above the Cave-Sandstone.

Nearly all the summer-rainfall species flower during the summer, but a few are autumn flowering, like the relatively newly discovered *P. laetans*, a rare endemic confined to the Blyde River escarpment. It is one of the more richly coloured of the otherwise comparatively drab summer-rainfall-region proteas.

laetans

1. *P. decurrens*

2. *P. laevis*

3. *P. cryophila*

4. *P. lorea*

mucronifolia

DWARF PROTEAS

Most proteas have fairly wide distribution ranges and are still moderately abundant in their natural habitats, but a few species, especially those from lowland sites, have become very rare. *Protea mucronifolia* is such an example. As its natural habitat falls within an area of intense agricultural development, *P. mucronifolia* had been almost completely exterminated by the middle of this century. Now restricted to a recently proclaimed private nature reserve and an adjacent farm in the Hermon-Gouda district north of Wellington, this tiny December-flowering species has happily been saved from certain extinction.

The other species shown here are dwarf, ground-flowering proteas, characterized by a low-tufted growth habit and flower heads borne at or near ground level. Several have underground stems – a feature which enables them to survive veld fires. Indeed, many of these species, like *P. lorea* from Helderberg and the Drakenstein mountains, flower most profusely on the new growth which sprouts from the underground stems in the aftermath of a veld fire.

Grandest of all is *P. cryophila*, the snow protea of the Cederberg. Its huge, woolly flower heads rival those of *P. cynaroides* in size. This very slow-growing species occurs in the high Cederberg, on Sneeuwkop, Sneeuwberg and Langberg among other sites – generally above 1 800 metres.

Protea laevis will also be seen by climbers in the Cederberg, in moist sites, between September and December.

In the dry hills around Worcester, *P. restionifolia* flourishes. Its concealed flower heads, surrounded by dull, velvety, brown bracts, are clearly not designed to attract bird pollinators, in the manner of many of its showy relatives. Instead, this species emits a musty-yeasty odour after sunset, which attracts nocturnally active rodents.

The rough-leaved *Protea aspera* is one of the more commonly encountered ground-flowering species, and occurs mainly between Hermanus and Bredasdorp.

estionifolia

7. P. aspera

9

1. *L. argenteum*

3. *L. singulare*

4. *L. gandogeri*

2. *L. floridum*

5. *L. salignum*

GENUS *LEUCADENDRON*

After *Protea*, *Leucadendron*, comprising 81 species, is the largest African genus of the Proteaceae. Unlike *Protea*, which extends its range into central, east and west Africa, *Leucadendron* is endemic to southern Africa. Moreover, apart from two outliers in southern Natal, the remaining species are massed in the south western and southern Cape.

Of all the Proteaceae, *Leucadendron* presents the greatest diversity of seed types. Some are hard, smooth and nut-like, others flat, black and papery, while still others are variously hairy or plumed. Associated with these different seed types are two quite different strategies which have been evolved for surviving fires. One method involves the retention of the mature seeds within a hard, woody cone. The seeds are only released when the shrub is damaged or killed by fire – a phenomenon known as 'serotiny'. The other involves the seeds being released a few months after the flowers have faded, to be carried off and safely buried by ants.

An immediately distinguishing feature of this genus is that the male and female flower heads are borne on separate plants. They are invariably tiny (seldom exceeding 25 millimetres in diameter), and are usually surrounded by a loose circlet of leaves which remain green for most of the year, but suddenly become suffused with rich, yellow tones as flowering commences. Common to the point of being ubiquitous, leucadendrons are among the glories of the *fynbos* in winter (their principal flowering time), illuminating the sombre veld with huge splashes of gold, buttery yellows or russety reds. A few, like *L. salignum*, take on crimson tones, especially in the Kouebokkeveld and Langkloof, where the winter frosts seem to sharpen and intensify the hues.

L. argenteum, the famous silver tree, can still be seen growing wild on Lion's Head, at Kirstenbosch and on Vlakkenberg, Constantia. Now cultivated in several temperate parts of the world for its remarkable silvery foliage – which remains this colour throughout the year – the silver tree, attaining up to 10 metres in height when mature, is the only *Leucadendron* which can truly be called a tree. The remaining species are shrubs, rarely exceeding four metres.

bonum

1. *L. cordatum*

2. *L. pubibracteolatum* (male)

3. *L. nervosum* 4. *L. pubibracteolatum* (female)

strobilinum

eucalyptifolium

6. *L. discolor*

All leucadendrons are known by the common names *geelbos* (yellow bush) and *tolbos* (top bush). The latter name refers to the hard, woody, usually oval seed-bearing cones that are characteristic of the female plants.

The fact that male and female flowers occur on separate plants ensures that cross-pollination takes place. A few leucadendrons (for example, *L. macowanii*) have a dry, powdery pollen which allows wind pollination, but the majority depend on a host of small flying insects to transport their sticky pollen.

Leucadendrons are found in almost every ecological niche in the *fynbos*. *Leucadendron cordatum*, with its nodding heads, favours the arid northern slopes of the Langeberg and Swartberg, while *L. strobilinum* requires the perpetually damp, shaded conditions found on the upper south slopes of Table Mountain. Others, like *L. eucalyptifoliam*, are more adaptable. This handsome species grows in dense thickets in the Langeberg and Outeniqua mountains, on both the dry northern slopes and the moist southern aspects.

A curious feature of this genus is that the male flower heads are generally more attractive and brightly pigmented than those of the female – as can be seen in the male and female *L. pubibracteolatum* shown here. The leaves surrounding the male heads are golden at flowering time, but remain grey-green in the female. Male flower heads in *L. discolor* are endowed with a cluster of brilliant-red male flowers within a yellow cup of surrounding leaves. Though very rare in its natural habitat on Piketberg, it is abundant in cultivation, and is an important item in the cut-flower trade. Because the preferred method of propagation is the cloning of superior male plants, female plants are seldom found in gardens.

1. *L. reflexum*

2. *L. mundii*   3. *L. gueinzii*

spathulatum

GENUS *LEUCOSPERMUM*

Unlike *Protea* and *Leucadendron*, which have solitary flower heads borne on ends of shoots, the flower head of a leucospermum grows in an axillary position, that is, between the upper surface of the branch and the stem. It faces towards the apex of the flowering shoot, and may be solitary or grouped. It is, however, the individual flowers comprising each head that really distinguish *Leucospermum* from *Protea* and *Leucadendron*. Well developed, with stout, spreading, brilliantly coloured styles, they create a spiky, pincushion-like effect in a fully open bloom, hence the leucospermum's popular name of 'pincushion'.

All 47 species of *Leucospermum* occur in the southern African region – the majority in the south western and southern Cape, although there are a few species which are peculiar to the summer-rainfall area. *Leucospermum gerrardii* (overleaf), for instance, is found in Natal, the highlands of Swaziland and the Eastern Transvaal.

One of the most widely cultivated and best-known species is *L. reflexum*, seen here in its natural habitat among the Cederberg mountains. Although it is usually bright scarlet, a pale-yellow colour variant is now becoming popular in gardens.

The *kreupelhout* (*L. concocarpodendron*), a tree still common on Table Mountain, was once a major source of fuel for the early settlers at the Cape. Its heavy bark was also a useful source of tannin.

Most other leucospermums are, however, shrubby – one to three metres tall – but not especially woody. *Leucospermum gueinzii*, a very localized species of the Hottentots Holland mountains, and *L. mundii*, which grows on the Langeberg between Zuurbraak and Riversdale, are typical examples. A few leucospermums have a prostrate, mat-like mode of growth – seen here in *L. spathulatum*, an uncommon species from the eastern Cederberg, and the sweetly scented *L. hypophyllocarpodendron*, once common on the sandy flats around Cape Town.

hypophyllocarpodendron

6. *L. conocarpodendron* (kreupelhout)

15

To many people, the Proteaceae are still 'wild flowers'. However, during the past few years, some genera have become prime subjects for domestication. *Leucospermum* species, with their vivid colours and long-lasting flowerheads, are especially popular, and hybrids between *L. cordifolium*, *L. tottum* and *L. glabrum* have been selected for specific characteristics to suit the local cut-flower trade, as well as export markets. They are a far cry from the wild species from which they were so recently bred. Leucospermums are clearly destined to join other South African plants, such as freesias, gladioli, pelargoniums and gerberas, as familiar garden subjects the world over.

Most of the larger-flowered leucospermums are bird pollinated, their wiry styles providing convenient perches for nectar-seeking birds, such as the Cape long-tailed sugarbird and various smaller sunbirds.

Several leucospermums display marked colour changes in the flower heads at different stages of their maturation. *L. gracile*, of the Hermanus mountains, and *L. mundii* provide good examples of this feature. Both open yellow, become orange-coloured after pollination, and eventually turn deep crimson as the seeds mature. Such colour changes are believed to provide visual cues to pollinators. The specific colour or hue of a flower tends to be most visually attractive to potential pollinators when the pollen is ripe and the female parts are at their most receptive.

Another fascinating aspect of leucospermums is that their seeds are ant-dispersed. The oval, greyish seeds mature rapidly as each flower head fades. When the spent bloom begins to disintegrate, the ripe seeds fall to the ground. They do not remain there long, but are gathered up within minutes by several different species of ant. Lured by a powerful chemical attractant in the fresh seed coat, the ants laboriously haul the newly fallen seeds away to underground seed caches, where they are safe from rodent predators. The ants appear to be interested only in the soft seed coat, leaving the hard, nut-like seed intact to germinate later, when conditions are suitable.

1. *L. tottum*

2. *L. profugum*

3. *L. lineare*

4. *L. gracile*

glabrum

6. L. fulgens

gerrardii

1. *M. hottentoticus*

GENUS *MIMETES*

Mimetes is probably the most beguiling of all the South African Proteaceae. Of the 13 species, only one, *M. cucullatus*, is widespread throughout the south western and southern Cape. The remainder are uncommon or very rare, and one, *M. stokoei*, is extinct. The majority favour moist, montane habitats: *M. hottentoticus*, for instance, is endemic to Kogelberg, a peak at the head of the Palmiet River valley.

Each flowering shoot is a spectacular structure which, though appearing to be a single flower head, is in fact formed from numerous small, axillary flower heads, congregated among the often richly coloured leaves terminating each shoot. Most *Mimetes* are shrubby, but two species, *M. fimbriifolius* (found only in the Cape Peninsula) and *M. arboreus* of the Kogelberg Reserve, are tree-like, attaining three to five metres. Autumn-flowering *M. arboreus* is silver-leaved, as is its shrubby relative, *M. argenteus*, from the Hottentots Holland mountains. The last of the silver-leaved trio is *M. splendidus*, which occurs sporadically on the upper southern slopes of the Langeberg. Its subtle, salmon-coloured blooms are produced from midwinter until early spring.

In *M. capitulatus*, an endangered species from Groenlandberg, Grabouw, it is the grotesquely ornamented orange styles and bright bracts enfolding each axillary cluster of flowers that provide the main display, rather than the leaves.

Although the majority of *Mimetes* occur within nature or forest reserves, populations of most species are small and very localized. They are naturally rare, and have probably been so ever since the advent of man. With the exception of *M. cucullatus* – the only species that has taken readily to cultivation – *Mimetes* have all proved difficult to maintain in gardens. Careful habitat management is therefore the only acceptable way of ensuring the future survival of these magnificent plants. Those wishing to view *Mimetes* in the field can now do so from several National Hiking Way trails that have recently been opened to the public.

2. *M. arboreus*

fimbriifolius

4. M. splendidus

capitulatus

6. M. argenteus

1. *Serruria rosea*

2. *Serruria florida* (blushing bride)

3. *Serruria glo*

...rruria rubricaulis

OTHER GENERA

The species shown on these pages belong to
three different genera, but because of their
similarity in appearance, they are not easily
distinguished by the non-botanist. *Serruria*
(about 65 species) can be told apart from
Spatalla (20 species) and *Sorocephalus* (11
species) by the fact that it has divided leaves,
while the other two have simple, heath-like or
needle-like leaves.

Of the serrurias, the blushing bride (*S.
florida*) is the most famous and admired. Once
nearly extinct in its natural habitat in the
Assegaaibos valley near Franschhoek, it was
brought into cultivation at Kirstenbosch in
1916, whence it was introduced to gardens in
several parts of the world. A related species,
the pink-flowered *S. rosea*, occurs in the
Wemmershoek mountains, also near
Franschhoek. When it is grown together with *S.
florida* in gardens, the two frequently hybridize,
producing very handsome offspring. Few other
serrurias have their flower heads enclosed in
papery bracts. Instead, their flowers are borne
in loosely branched clusters, like *S. rubricaulis*
and *S. glomerata*. The latter is endemic to the
Cape Peninsula.

Many species of *Serruria* which previously
occurred in lowland habitats such as the Cape
Flats have disappeared, as a result of urban
development. Others survive only in botanic
gardens or in small, isolated remnants of
fynbos.

Spatalla has tiny flowers, curved forward in
cylindrical or spike-like heads, while
Sorocephalus produces straight flowers in
rounded or oval heads. Both genera tend to
favour high montane habitats. Because their
species are invariably rare and very local in
their distribution, they are seldom seen.
Spatalla caudata, one of the more easily
observable species, grows on damp seepage
areas in the Kouebokkeveld, while
Sorocephalus clavigerus is occasionally
encountered in the Steenbras, Kleinmond
and Hottentots Holland mountains.

...ocephalus clavigerus

6. *Spatalla caudata*

1. *Aulax cancellata*

2. *Diastella divaricata*

3. *Vexatorella latebrosa*

4. *Brabejum stellatifolium* (wild almond)

5. *Orothamnus zeyheri* (marsh rose)

anomus sceptrum-gustavianus

rea saligna (boekenhout)

Protea, Leucadendron, Leucospermum and *Serruria* are the largest genera of the Proteaceae in southern Africa, but some of the smaller, lesser-known groups – shown here – are equally attractive.

Aulax (three species), like *Leucadendron*, produces male and female flowers on separate plants. The male flowers have loosely arranged, yellow, plume-like spikes, while the female blooms are borne within a woody cup.

There are seven species of *Diastella*, most of which are soft, herbaceous shrublets producing tiny (10-20 millimetres in diameter), pink or white flowers almost continuously throughout the year.

Vexatorella (three species) is represented by the recently described *V. latebrosa*, a rare, localized species from the Langeberg near Robertson.

Brabejum has only a single species, *B. stellatifolium*, the wild almond, so called because its bitter, inedible fruits resemble almonds. Jan van Riebeeck, first commander of the Cape, planted a hedge of these trees along Wynberg Hill in 1660 to demarcate the settlement's boundary. Parts of the hedge still survive there.

Most of the 18 species of *Paranomus* have divided leaves, but a few have the curious habit of producing two leaf-forms on the same plant – divided leaves on the lower branches and entire leaves on the upper branches. It is presumably because of this that the genus was named *Paranomus*, meaning 'not according to the rules'. Most of the genus favours montane habitats: for instance, *P. sceptrum-gustavianus* of the Hottentots Holland mountains.

Orothamnus zeyheri, the famous marsh rose, grows in the Kogelberg Reserve, at Betty's Bay and in the Hermanus mountains. Although this species was once in serious danger of extinction, several populations have been revitalized by means of carefully researched veld-management programmes.

Faurea (four species in South Africa) is a genus of small trees occurring mainly in savannah woodland in the Transvaal and Natal. Commonest is *F. saligna*, the *boekenhout*, which can easily be mistaken for a eucalyptus when not in flower. With their long, loose, rather simple, spike-like flower heads of dull, greenish-brown flowers, faureas are thought to represent the most primitive living genus of the Proteaceae in Africa.

ANIMAL POLLINATION

Birds, insects and rodents are among the animals responsible for the vital process of cross-pollination in the Proteaceae.

Most obvious are birds such as the Cape long-tailed sugarbird, as well as the orange-breasted, lesser double-collared, and malachite sunbirds. They are active during daylight hours, probing flower heads of *Protea*, *Leucospermum* and *Mimetes*. When they plunge their bills into open flower heads in the search for nectar, pollen accumulates on their foreheads and is later rubbed off onto receptive areas of the erect stigmas when the action is repeated on another flower head.

Nocturnal rodents, especially the Namaqua rock mouse, lap nectar from the cryptically concealed flower heads of ground-flowering species like *Protea humiflora* and, in so doing, cover their snouts with pollen. When another bloom is visited, the pollen is transferred to the receptive stigmas.

While bird and rodent pollination may well be phenomena that have evolved fairly recently, hairy scarab beetles are ancient, long-established pollinators of some of the summer-rainfall-area proteas, which have shallow, saucer-shaped flowers; *P. welwitschii* and *P. caffra*, for instance.

1. Malachite sunbird on *Leucospermum cordifolium*

2. Cape sugarbird on *Leucospermum cordifolium*

3. Namaqua rock mouse on *Protea humiflora*

4. Scarab beetle on *Protea multibracteata*